Ghosts Still Linger

Ghosts Still Linger

KAT CAMERON

UNIVERSITY of ALBERTA PRESS

Published by

1–16 Rutherford Library South
11204 89 Avenue NW
Edmonton, Alberta, Canada T6G 2J4
uap.ualberta.ca

LIBRARY AND ARCHIVES CANADA
CATALOGUING IN PUBLICATION

Title: Ghosts still linger / Kat Cameron.
Names: Cameron, Kat, 1964– author.
Series: Robert Kroetsch series.
Description: Series statement: Robert
    Kroetsch series | Poems.
Identifiers: Canadiana (print) 20190239182 |
    Canadiana (ebook) 20190239255 |
    ISBN 9781772125092 (softcover) |
    ISBN 9781772125207 (PDF)
Classification: LCC PS8605.A4818 G46 2020 |
    DDC C811/.6—dc23

First edition, first printing, 2020.
First printed and bound in Canada by
Houghton Boston Printers, Saskatoon,
Saskatchewan.
Copyediting and proofreading by
Jenna Butler.

A volume in the Robert Kroetsch Series.

University of Alberta Press gratefully
acknowledges the support received for its
publishing program from the Government
of Canada, the Canada Council for the Arts,
and the Government of Alberta through the
Alberta Media Fund.

For Derrick
remembering a week in Wyoming

Contents

LIGHTNING OVER WYOMING

Ghosts are Ordinary

I suppose that ghosts are ordinary
and must resemble what they will not leave.

—RICHARD GREENE, "Over the Border"

Cracked

If we're cracked open,
it's only because something wants out.
——ANNE SIMPSON, "Winter"

Imagine her in 1916, a child in a tanned
hide jacket with three-quarter-length sleeves,
brass and plastic buttons, fringes
and glass beads. There are no pictures.
She always effaced herself
in photos, one hand shielding her eyes,
wavering at the edge of family.
If we're cracked open

all the stories spill out. But there are no stories,
only a four-year-old girl and her little buddy
in the years of the Great War.
She reappears in 1935,
now wife and mother, all stories silenced.
She was never quite there.
Cracked, the roles rubbed thin—
because something wants out.

Blue Scarf

Before the funeral, her daughters
invite us into the bedroom.
Heaped high on the bed,
all the scarves she'd worn:
blue cotton, red silk, purple polyester,
bright twisted yarn, green and white checks,
printed birds and flowers.

I remember the summer of 2011,
the square kerchief printed with the Canadian flag.
When we arrived in South River,
Bea came out on the deck, beaming, her hair,
thinned by chemo, hidden under the flag.
On Canada Day, surrounded by grandchildren,
she is the centre of every picture, smiling,
her arthritic hands bent backwards at the wrist.

I choose a blue the colour of her eyes.

Later, in the church,
each niece is wrapped
in the sign of mourning.

B-Flat Minor

A Don Draper kind of man

—PAOLO PIETROPAOLO

B-flat minor is tormented. He drinks whiskey
straight, still smokes, although he's trying to quit.

B-flat minor is Rachmaninoff's *Concerto #2*,
all romantic nonsense and bluster.

He's a man from the fifties, a clean-shave anachronism,
but these men still exist, wallowing in furtive affairs,

so assured that they're the ones women want,
when really, we're searching for A major,

Copland's *Appalachian Spring*, that light touch,
and the promise of simple gifts.

Lament

For John Mann (1962–2019)

His words are gone,
    eaten by Alzheimer's. Remember running
from stage to stage? Hula girls swirling,

dust on our feet, dragonflies darting.
    The way he danced,
flailing, joyous. Canada mourns for one bard sinking

down into darkness, scalped tickets in Kingston,
    but I am grieving
the last Commodore concert, when he read his words

from an iPad screen. Remember dancing
    to the beat of the bodhran?
His words are gone, but John Mann dances.

Haunted

I.

After all this time, I am a ghost to you.
You're on an island, writing poems.

You wanted to be free of memory,
the sooty slash of absence in your poems.

Old loves fall away like rotting trees
or drift like flotsam in the ocean's foam.

After all this time, I am a ghost to you.
You are an island, writing poems.

II.

Black mast and black sails swollen with wind—
slashed kanji of the heart's stylized shell.

Breathe in cathedral trees, columns of light.
Buried in bracken, fragments of a snail's shell.

A necklace pieced from seed pearls, gold,
sorrow, and a painted sapphire shell.

The room has been emptied—chair and table,
bureau, bed. Nothing left but memory's shell.

III.

You shredded papers, sorted through old clothes.
You kept my pink shirt. You always cried.

So little that we own holds meaning. Think of death
as a slow shedding of possessions. You often cried.

Over grey spume, white clouds drift:
crumpled fragments of paper. A seagull's cry.

If I call, you won't reply. You cannot hear
me through the gate of time. You seldom cry.

IV.

Tired of grief, I want to spend a month
alone, watching the crescent wax and wane.

Anger. Denial. Acceptance. Filter through
the pain. Emotions ebbing through wax and wane.

Shaking Quakers danced with ecstasy, struck
by a bolt of light. My belief waxes and wanes.

I watch the Pleiades shine in the sky's
unseeing dome. Gutted by the work of wax and wane.

v.

Water drips from stones arches, a hint of rot.
The walls are closing in. At the end is a light.

I'm driving down a lane lined with hedges starred
with golden flowers. At the end is a light.

Green fields. Open gate. Over the border, what
awaits? I need to know. At the end is a light.

What lies ahead? Darkness? The promised land?
Soon I will know. At the end is a light.

VI.

I rarely cry. Rain drifts for hours—
an eternity of grey on the other side.

Unmade bed. I sleep alone. If I fall
asleep, will I wake on the other side?

The sun comes out, light breaking in bright
shards. What falls away is on the other side:

your body. Gone. Kat translates grief
into black-edged letters on the other side.

For Gerda, on the threshold

> the thing that cannot happen,
> happens, the thing that no one sees:
> some place past emptiness
> we take another step.
> —JAN ZWICKY, "Beethoven: Op. 95"

A slow decline
for fifteen years. First, the tremor—
fears of a brain tumour. Then loss
of balance, shakiness, memory slips,
and the diagnosis: Parkinson's disease.
The beginning of the end,
dopamine fails,
signals switch off, and cells die,
but still we ignore what is coming, pretend
the thing that cannot happen.

She weeps often. She rarely wept
when I was young. Is it
the drug's ebb
and flow, or her anger at
the body's broken machinery?
Shaking hands, stalled feet. She
tries to hide her symptoms, embarrassed,
trapped in the spotlight of care,
fights on as the disease
happens, the thing that no one sees.

On tiptoes, she shuffles
down the hall, a stutter of muscles
spasming. She holds my hands,
a toddler again, unsteady,
needing encouragement.
On the threshold, she pauses,
fearing
that dim liminal
space, but we all dread unknowingness—
some place past emptiness.

Not knowing what waits
on the other side of the door,
we pause for a moment,
teetering, unsure,
as a person on the other side
coaxes us through:
and on that far
side, in darkness or
a loving spotlight,
we take another step.

Paper Chambers

She cries so easily now, over her dead sisters, how she is a burden.
When I was young, she would collage Valentine poems onto paper hearts. Now
her hand trembles, curls into a claw. She can't write her name on birthday cards,
that smooth cursive. She says, "I can't make my body work," and her words
rip my heart's paper chambers.

Windows of Faith

My grandma claimed she could see ghosts.
    One night in the summer of 1927,
after her father-in-law had died of septicemia
from an infected cut on his foot,
    the dog started barking.
Mr. Craig stood
    by the gate
at the end of the lane.

My dad has a touch of second sight.
At the Commonwealth Games,
    he knew that the Russian diver
would fall. Did he read
the body's language, a brief hesitation;
was it intuition?
    Or did he hear the crack of skull
a fraction before the crowd?

On a June evening in England, we
heard, or thought we heard,
    singing in the ruins
    of Fountains Abbey:
lush lawns and grey gothic spires,
    windows of faith knocked out,
illuminated by fading crimson sky.

Bastille Day 2016

The cathedral in Madrid reeks of blood,
stone walls stained with damp and history.

Clotted red windows of stained glass turn
the light a murk that candles cannot pierce.

Despite the coins dropped into metal slots,
the ghosts still linger. We cannot buy them off.

In the Prado, frame after frame of tortured men:
elongated El Greco saints, tinged

with green, looking slightly more dead than
real corpses, strung up for our attention—

Christo Muerto, oozing black blood.
Old wounds splattered in paint—

bodies sheeted on the beach
by the Mediterranean Sea.

The King in the Car Park

But I am in
So far in blood that sin will pluck on sin.
—SHAKESPEARE, *The Tragedy of King Richard the Third*

Poor Richard, villain, hunchback, murderer,
has been unearthed, his bones lost for 400 years

after the battle of Bosworth Field
until archaeologists plotted the site

of Grey Friars, dissolved by that Tudor
who killed his wives, rather than his nephews.

DNA tests confirm that it is Richard,
killed August 22, 1485.

King for only two years. Challenged by
Henry Tudor, Senior, that Welsh upstart,

he rode off to war with allies who waited
on the flanks, sensing a change in dynasties.

Knowing the battle was lost, he charged
and was pulled down, crying *"A horse! a horse!"*

Displayed, then buried in an unmarked grave,
he lay beneath concrete and cars.

Human remains—how often we unearth
the past. What do the bones tell us?

The body, twisted with scoliosis,
curls in the cavity, unshrouded, uncoffined,

a Roman nail embedded in the ribs.
Ten wounds to the skull, two fatal, made by

a halberd that sliced through to the other side.
The rebuilt skull—a facsimile of

sharp nose, Beatles hair, pursed lips.
The face of an ascetic, not a monster.

Everything adds up: Richard Crookback,
one shoulder higher than the other,

unhorsed, killed by a Welsh foot soldier,
hacked into the mud of Bosworth Field.

History is written by the victors, and
Shakespeare painted the picture that lasted:

Richard, villainized in widows' voices,
"I had a Harry, till a Richard killed him."

The truth is still lost. *I'm telling you stories.*

A Diary

And so I am reading Pepys, that hypocrite,
blackening his wife's eye and then nipping
down to the tavern to fondle Bess,
the serving wench, and recording all of it—

his morning coffee, books bought, sums earned,
his amours, written in Latin shorthand,
meetings with his patron, Lord Sandwich,
(such a name), hangovers, the king, profits turned.

Pepys, in the year 1665, wanders
the streets during the plague, notes red crosses
on doors, bodies removed at night,
over six thousand dead, and he ponders,

how empty the streets are and melancholy.
All through the summer, he listens to bells
tolling each death (except Quakers and Jews)
yet remarks he feels *the greatest joy.*

He exhibits an untroubled conscience—
in December writes, *thus ends this year,*
to my great joy, before he adds up his profits
his estate increased through diligence;

he ends, *Pray God continue the plague's decrease,*
but only so the court may return.

Alberta Advantage

Athabasca Glacier 1924

BLUE

Harris saw blue. Sheets of
ice, colossal geometry:

a triangle, a rhomboid. On a
blank page of snow,

he slashed lines of primal colour,
more than a glacier, primitive,

mysteries encapsulating
form. His indigo glows.

WHITE

A photograph of the six-week expedition
shows four pack horses crossing an expanse

of clear white, hock-deep in snow,
led by a silhouetted cowboy in chaps.

Harmon composed the shot in F-stops—white
made visible by the crenellations

of the dark peaks behind, a bowl of light
spilling outward to fill the frame.

GREY

We saw grey, an ancient tortoise shell
scored with lines and fissures,

dated concrete markers mapping
an accelerating glacial retreat.

The ice cracks and shrinks,
disappearing into memory.

Big Burn

September 2, 1666. Watching from a river boat,
Pepys describes the Great Fire, *the most horrid malicious*
bloody flame destroying London, houses pulled down
to stop the fire's spread, records how people *remove*
their goods and leave all to the fire—
  he and his neighbour dig a *pit and put*
our wine in it; and I my Parmesan cheese.

August 1910. The Big Burn engulfs
three million acres in Idaho, Washington, and Montana,
kills seventy-eight firefighters, flattens Henderson,
Taft, Falcon, Grand Forks, Haughan,
  traps Ed Pulaski and forty-five men
for five hours. Pulaski blankets the mouth
of the cave, threatens to shoot anyone attempting to escape,
  saves all but five men.

May 3, 2016. The Beast jumps the river into Fort Mac,
razes houses, a hotel, a hill
of pines— fireballs of flame.
  Highway 63 a runway of red tail lights.
What to save?
Divorce papers. Snow pants and cheese slices.
Two teenagers ride their horses
  north of town.

Copper Moon

On a country road,
out of the heat haze
   a harvest moon, copper

as it breaks the horizon,
then round and white
   over bright canola.

Crickets clicking in the twitch,
   mosquitoes
and one crumpled Budweiser can

silver and red
in a ditch filled with cattails
   and stagnant water.

Summer night
   manure and mist.

Drought

Thirty days with no rain
rip holes into the boreal forest
hiding the horizon. Last week
soared in the sky
gutting lives

the northern fires
a bright wall of flame
a scarlet wyrm
backlit by choking smoke
grey ash.

Elms

I mourn the loss of every tree.
The elms that lined the avenue are gone—
that green inverted sea.
I mourn the loss of every tree,

cathedral memory
stripped to ruin.
I mourn the loss of every tree—
the elms that lined the avenue are gone.

Flood Erasures 2013

Erasure poem from *Cottonopolis*

The air closed in. Breaking storm.
The ground's so wet, soaked.

What can you do?
We asked, we waited.

Everything we had: books, clock, clothes,
shoes, chairs. Sleeping bag on the floor.

Line up, tired and quiet. Go back home. Or just—
no. It's like that, feel it, see it in the eyes.

Nothing but a couple of empty jars—

Sunny at last. Such rain!
The clouds were black

and then today, sun. Stand up. Wind
and the cold sun. The breeze.

See, not much left,
a jar of water.

Garden

Il faut cultiver notre jardin.

—VOLTAIRE, *Candide*

The flowering of fifty years:
three walls of fence, the shaded grass,
lilies unfolding sunshine tips,
    apple tree with tiny pips,
Johnny-jump-ups, iris stalks.
    Clover scintillates
with dew. Dandelions spread their grip,
serrated leaves, taproot deep.
On the rotting deck,
    missing boards gap.

Down the block a persistent thud—
where a house once stood
    a maw of mud.

Hinton 2013

A highway town, curving down
to the sawmill by the river
    and curving up again.

On Sunday, the town smells of pulp
and a faint haze of smoke from forests
burning in Nordegg and Lodgepole.

Smoke drifts across the province:
    three summers of drought,
a century of human arrogance.

Families in F-150s crowd
into the Tims drive-through
for donuts and double-doubles.

Trucks and Timbits, currency
    of Alberta prosperity.

Interlude

Slick sheen in alleys
after a chinook blows through—
January rain.

Powdery white snow,
dipped
in February's glaze.

March comes in—a Lion Dance
with clashing cymbals.

Johnston Canyon

Snap on crampons for the ice walk,
the ground slick below our boots.

Solstice, low sun on the horizon: an hour
for this hike. We follow a snow-packed path

through pines, onto catwalks fastened
to granite heights, icicles hung from rock.

At the end, a low-roofed stone passage
opens on an uneven ledge revealing

a pool of water, frothing emerald green,
shining with light. The whirlpool

rimmed by frozen falls, clear sheen
of ice, fresh powder, a skiff of snow,

water coating the rocks, frozen
in rivulets dripping down the ice.

K-Country

for Dad, who taught me to canoe

The Lower Lake, glacier run-off icy on my feet,
holding the canoe as Dad balanced his way back
to the stern, my sister sat on the life-jacket
in the thwart, and I stepped in at the bow, pushing off
with my paddle's grip, soft moss cushioning the keel.
We paddled to the drowned caves, the washed-out dens
of disinherited bears banished by the dam's flood,
white ghosts of tree stumps submerged below our wake,
the smooth pull, water dripping from the blades,
and the curlews' call echoing from the shore.

Years later, I brought a friend to K-Country.
We went canoeing, an August day, the lake
as still as in past years, unchanged,
a mountain sky clear in the moment between storms,
and he asked, "Do you feel lucky?" I knew
he meant all this, the cabin, the lake, the parents
who taught me to canoe, the mountains
cradling this place.

Loons and Wolf Willows

I know each curve, the paved road through
the trees—white spruce, larches—down a hill
to the moose meadow, a muskeg bowl

between two ridges, turn right at the dead-end sign
(magician's ward) onto a road that s-curves
past A-frames morphing into two-story chalets

of steel and glass, to the cabin on the steep hill.
Kin-oh-ah-kis. Stoney word for meeting of the waters.
In 1960, my grandma entered a lottery, won a plot

where chinook winds shush through swaying
lodgepole pines, and we would go every summer,
although the road wasn't paved until 1976

when Kananaskis Provincial Park was created.
I remember the drive, five hours in the back
of a green station wagon, dust billowing

on the gravel road, to two rooms, an outhouse,
water sloshed into ten-gallon tin cans from a pump
fifty feet up the road, until we drilled a well.

Grizzlies, black bears, moose, elk, white-tailed deer;
herds of bighorns licking salt on the highway;
lynx prints on the roof, cougars (never seen);

mountain goats—distant ghosts at Highwood Pass;
a route of wolves at midnight, leaping past headlights
in the falling snow, chasing Appaloosa ponies.

The Lower Lake, glacier-fed, forty metres deep,
blue-green, opaque, black below the mountain, high
in the fall, low in the spring, when it powers

the Pocaterra Dam. We'd canoe on the east side,
sandpipers and killdeer darting on the rocky shore,
beach the canoe, bushwack through wolf willows,

weaving our way on elk paths, spongy black-spruce
bog hummocked beneath our feet, and climb,
climb the steep dirt trail. Whiskey jacks, blue jays,

chickadees flitting in the trees,
ruby-throated hummingbirds sipping from the feeder
hung on the deck. The kitchen windows

looked west on clumped clouds of summer storms
crowding over the four peaks: Indefatigable.
Invincible. Black Prince. Warspite.

Warship names for the Shining Mountains
imprinted on my DNA. The loon's requiem
as the sun sets.

Moose Photobomb

One round brown eye looming in the lens,
the mountains' comic clown, shaggy eyebrows,
snout elongated like a tuba, lanky legs
tottery with a teenager's knobby joints,
the stumblebutt of nature's sitcoms.

Give us a wink. You're in on the joke;
you know we're watching. Put on a show.

Old North Trail

I will drive now to Innisfail
and stay at the Super 8 Motel
where old men smoke darts dispensed

from vintage vending machines in
the Stagecoach Saloon, panelled in knotty pine,
and the road crews swill Big Rock beer

and dream of their wives in double-wide trailers
set in yards overgrown with lilacs and caragana.

I will drive up the Old North Trail,
the same trail my great-great-grandparents
followed in 1891—that spring

the Red Deer River flooded, the men
missed the ford and foundered, a horse drowned,
and a loaded wagon floated downstream

with a young man clinging to his possessions.
The silted river flows into the present,

and at the Innisfail Rodeo, farmers decked out
in checked shirts, cowboy hats, and jeans
sit in the bleachers, forecasting the barometer

in Swedish, French, English, and German,
and their kids perch on the rails and pet the horses,
and the parking lot behind the grounds is crammed

with millions of dollars in fifth wheels and RVs
from cattle and oil in God's country.

Oilers Nation

Rig pigs and kids in orange and blue vestments
    jam Churchill Square in their thousands,

an exhilarated mass of playoff celebration, hockey
    their religion, the arena their temple,

breathing together, an hour of cheering, symbiosis
    of vowels. Hours later, the acolytes gather

in the forum, mosaic floor shaking
    from their stamping, *he shoots/he scores,*

their call and response, and when the game ends
    and the season is over, they still believe

this time next year.

Poetic Licence

Found poem on Alberta bumper stickers

Let the Eastern bastards freeze in the dark!

I heart Alberta beef.

Please, God, give us another oil boom,
    we promise not to piss it away again.

We've pissed it away again.

Caribou, not coal mines.
Coal mines don't belong in our sacred headwaters.

No fracking way.

Fuck off, we're full.
Still in Edmonton.

Prairie Fields

Tattered ghosts rising
above corduroy prairie fields,
golden haze of dust.

Evenings of endings:
last call, last song. The harvest
moon looms on the horizon.

Rollerblades

Low tide—the scavengers are out on Whyte,
checking the bins filled with empties
after a typical night.

A picker wearing rollerblades
rummages through Tim Hortons cups,
pulls out a plastic one-litre jug
of chocolate milk, pours out the liquid,
and stashes his find in a shopping cart.

He sets off fast, low-slung on skates,
probably played hockey,
moved north to the rigs,
    hit a snag—
drink, disease, drugs,
lost his job, his house, his way.

Urban magpies pick up debris
like mudlarks on the banks of the Thames
who scavenged for scraps
of coal and copper
in the raw sewage of the river.

Saturday Night Prowl

My cousin's doppelgänger
prowls the stage, howls the words
to "Enter Sandman"
in governed rage. Small-town dreams

shot, short-lived bands gone,
bottles of wine downed,
spliffs smoked—
gut-wrenched.

Still the menace in his stalk,
the could-have-been presence,

but
he pissed out
his talent
in the parking lot.

Territory

For Sale—a million-dollar cedar chalet near the weedy water of Half Moon Lake. Geese dive, tails like ruffled paintbrushes. Nine o'clock. A bloody sun setting behind the pines. Red-winged blackbirds sway on cattails. A dog barks, twice, a car appears in a haze of dust, and a couple strolls down the lane, patrolling their territory. A second pair of geese lands, and the first male flares his wings, driving them off. Antiphonal creaking of frogs, a squeaky hinge.

Until Help Arrives

Two years after the pre-dawn call, a white
  truck slams into a parked Mazda 3,

two doors from our house. A man convulses
  in his seat. A stranger holds his hand,

says, "I'm here, buddy," until the ambulance
  arrives. Later, all wreckage is gone—

towed truck, flatbed for the crumpled car,
  flashing red and blue lights stilled.

Disaster descends, and then dissipates,
  leaving charged nerves.

After the phone call, I held you as you wept,
  your world convulsed.

VW Ramblings

Found poem on a VW bus

Check ego. Pay attention.
I'm diagonally parked in a parallel universe.

Where are we going? Jerome, Arizona.
Grow your own dope. I need the money.
No guts, no glory. Go for it. It's the scenic route.

Why am I in this handbasket?
Don't make me release the flying monkeys.
Bring back the wolf. Plant a man.

My family is a freak show. I refuse to grow up,
but I'm open to change. Elvis Presley died for your sins.
Sometimes I wake up grouchy. Other times I let him sleep.

We are all here because we are not all there. You can't be first,
but you can be next. No one is ugly at 2 a.m.
Thanks for honking, now piss off.

No one died when Clinton lied. Question the answers.
Are we having fun yet? Every breath is a gift.
Have you runed your day yet?

Actions speak louder than bumper stickers.
Attitude makes the difference.

Whyte Avenue 2 a.m.

Each night, sirens sound on Whyte,
    pulsing jazz of red and blue.

Morning brings the body count—
    side-street stabbing,

bike crushed under car,
    restaurant razed by fire.

The party strobes the night—
    marauders smashing through.

YEG/YYC

Two dust-dry boomtowns.

Tyrannosaurus. Brontosaurus. Albertosaurus.

Two frontier cowboys trying to piss
on the biggest territory.

Long-legged construction cranes stalk
      prairie horizons.

Lightning over Wyoming

> and what i want to know is
> how do you like your blueeyed boy
> Mister Death
> — e.e. cummings, "[Buffalo Bill's]"

Man of the West

William "Buffalo Bill" Cody (1846–1917)

The hologram wavers in the first room
of the museum, a bearded man
wearing a grey suit and a white Stetson.
He welcomes us to his mausoleum

of history, his stagecoach, Wild West
posters festooned with his smiling face,
his buffalo stickpin in a glass case,
the most famous showman of the west.

This tomb to the afterlife has the booty
of the Pharaohs: costumes, jewelry,
paeans of praise. The *blue-eyed boy*
memorialized in the name of the city.

Look through his transparent image. Listen
to the vanished voices behind him.

Louisa's Locket

Louisa Maude Frederici Cody (1843–1921)

Those long flowing locks
    that high forehead
        the Vandyke beard.

Preserved in a locket
    in a glass case
        in a museum in Cody.

Lockets for memories
    lockets for hair
        and matching portraits.

Only his photo
    framed by mementoes
        from his dreams.

He was always away
    killing buffalo
        killing her dreams.

Taken

Kit Carson Cody (1870–1876)
Orra Maude Cody (1872–1883)

So little is left of children who die young—
a photograph, a lock of hair.
The son, Kit, dead of scarlet fever
at five. Wide, innocent eyes
and long blond ringlets.
When he died, Cody wrote to his sister,
"God has taken from us *our only* little boy."

The second daughter, Orra Maude,
dead at eleven.
She scowls at the camera
in her black dress
and striped stockings. Typhoid,
scarlet fever, accidents:
all those dead children of the plains.

White Shoes

Arta Cody Boal Thorp (1866–1904)

Her story a side show—a few photos
and a pair of satin shoes in a glass case.

White shoes for weddings.

Buffalo Bill wore thigh-high leather boots
in publicity photos of the great Army scout.

Leather boots for freedom.

She married young—her first husband's suicide
buried in the footnotes of her father's life.

White shoes for weddings.

When her father filed for divorce,
Arta wrote, *My heart is just broken over it.*

Leather boots for freedom.

She died in 1904, one month after
her second marriage.

Black dresses for funerals.

Woman in White

Irma Louisa Cody Garlow (1883–1918)

A woman in white haunts
the Irma Hotel in Cody,
the town Buffalo Bill built.

The last child, a last chance
at family harmony.

A sandstone hotel in her name,
a husband,
three children. A full life

until the Spanish flu killed her
and her husband, leaving more
motherless children for Louisa to raise.

Testimony

A dark-eyed young woman from St. Louis;
a handsome scout in the Civil War.

He said he rescued her from a runaway horse.
She was silent.

Tall tales and silence marked the marriage.

He built a town named Rome,
but the railway passed him by.

She said he was a failure.

She returned to St. Louis with their daughter.
He shot buffalo for two years on the plains.

He said they had their little differences.

II. DIVORCE

A melodrama of the Wild West. Newspapers ran headlines.

He said she poisoned him with Dragon's Blood.
She said, *I will rule Cody or ruin him.*

He said she was *a woman as cold blooded as a frog.*
She busted up the hotel rooms where he stayed with his mistresses.

The judge sided with Louisa. No divorce.

III. RECONCILIATION

They reconciled at the Welcome Wigwam
in North Platte, Nebraska, in 1911:

after the deaths of three children,
after the mistresses, the trial,
after claims of cruelty and poison.
Never for only a while, forever or not at all.

In a last photo, he is still the showman,
long hair under a hat, fringed buckskin,
high leather boots. She is a stout matron
in a black dress. His hand on her shoulder.

Soiled Doves

Whiskey Row in Prescott before the year
of the fire. Sealed rooms reeking of whiskey,
sweat, cigars, Florida water and spilled beer.

The census for the turn of the century
lists the boarders in a two-storey brothel—Jenny,
Mollie, Mary, Alba, Lulu, and another Mary.

The "housekeeper" was named Irish Annie.
No husband. Two wives, two widows.
Mary Two had an infant son, Henry.

These women lived in society's shadows,
documented only in census lies,
archeological mementoes.

Prairie nymphs, soiled doves, red-light ladies,
the fallen angels were denizens
of the cribs between Granite and Hades.

From an excavated privy on Lot 7:
ninety-six bottles for champagne, soda, wine,
hair dye, perfume, and laudanum;

a thunder mug, twenty-five buttons,
six toothbrushes, toothpaste jars, a shoe,
a hat, a doll's head, and a bone fan.

Misery and money on Whiskey Row
went hand in hand, but currency notes
were scarce, so the brothel known

as Kates Place in Prescott handed out
tin to pay for women who left no trace
but the tokens—circles with a cut-out

hole below the name, and a necklace
strung with Valentine hearts on a dotted chain.
Now trinkets for tourists, sold in this place

that once sold women who went insane,
took laudanum, survived, died.
A woman's body pared down, exchanged
for a tin circle.

Little Sure Shot

Annie Oakley Butler (1860–1926)

Born Phoebe Ann Mosey in a log cabin,
sixth of nine children. Two sisters died. One brother died.
Her father, caught in a blizzard, died.

Trapping at seven, hunting at eight, abandoned at nine
to a foster family she called "the wolves,"
starved, mistreated, locked out in the snow,

she escaped at eleven, found refuge
in Darke County Infirmary, learned
to read, to embroider, to survive.

Met Frank Butler in Cincinnati
when she was fifteen or twenty-one.

In the arena, she shot cigarettes and coins
from her trusting husband's hand. Some women
wished she would miss.

Miss Annie Oakley dressed like a lady
in hand-sewn dresses, embroidered in wild roses.

Shooting over her shoulder, her eyes fixed
on a mirror, she sliced playing cards
in half. Smashed glass targets shot into the air:
nine hundred in eight hours.

At five foot nothing, she was no threat
to the men who complimented her
on her "ladylike manner."

Would the act have worked
if she hadn't skipped into the arena
blowing kisses, if she hadn't done
that cute little kick at the end of each show?

An image cultivated as carefully
as a homesteader's garden.

Glass Targets in a Museum

They always put women behind glass.

Annie smashed hundreds—amber or cobalt blue,
mold-blown by Agnew & Brown,

exploding in a shower of feathers
and sawdust that coated the crowds below.

In a shooting contest, she beat
Frank Butler by one shot

to win a hundred-dollar bet,
but *Annie Get Your Gun* changes

    the story: she loses.
Annie, keep breaking those spheres

above our heads—targets clear as glass—
    no tricks, no lies.

Annie's Gun

Sometimes I want a gun. Freud said
a woman wants a penis, but only a dick
would believe this. A penis is a limp sack
of flesh, laughable at times, appealing
when rampant, but really, not the raw pack
of power that some men seem to think.

No, we want a gun. Annie knew this,
with her customized Lancaster rifle,
her silver initials on the stock, the gun
an extension of herself, obliterating
society's blue glass balls: orphan, wham!
poor, wham! woman, wham!
With a flash from the rifle, she
smashed her social carapace.

Lightning over Wyoming

The world is lit by lightning.
—TENNESSEE WILLIAMS, *The Glass Menagerie*

I.

Northern Wyoming
a lightning storm over Devils Tower
    that looming cone
    sandblasted by centuries

grey hexagonal columns
    a volcanic laccolith.

That night, sheets
    of bright white

bannered behind the tower.
Negative charges of electricity
    flashing through
an ionized path—

visible kinetic energy
    luminous echoes.

II.

Gazing on Mont Blanc

Shelley wrote
   the power is there
   although the man

who inscribed "Shelley, philanthropist,
poet, atheist" in a hotel guestbook

 was unlikely to see God's hand
      forming the universe.

Hiking around the curve
      of the tower
      we saw pieces of cloth

prayer bundles in red, yellow, black and white—
      colours of the four directions—
      tied to the branches of ponderosa pine.

The space is sacred to the Lakota, off-limits in June
      but flashes of red spandex moved

across the pillared face, defying belief.

Above, the black wingspans of five turkey vultures
        riding the updrafts
        punctuated blue sky.

III.

In Buffalo, we stopped
        for Rocky Road ice-cream
        at a booth on Main Street.

The hard-eyed owner told us, "In August
the rally brings over half a million bikers
        from Sturgis, South Dakota."

She and her husband set up
a Ministry for Motorcycles booth.

The line of bikes looped around
        the tower's base
        a noose circling a neck.

Our draw was *Close Encounters of the Third Kind*
Richard Dreyfus building mud mountains

        those five haunting notes.

We thought of bringing mashed potatoes
        posing for pictures.

IV.

Devils Tower
　　a dissonant shape
　　in a flat landscape

inspiring wonder, but interpretations
are only approximations.

The universe of things is

piles of rubble, broken columns
strewn around the tower's base
　　a fallen city.

This monolith
　　illuminated
　　by banners of light

a kaleidoscope of images—

fragmentary flashes.

Notes

The epigraph is from Richard Greene's *Boxing the Compass*, Signal Editions, 2009.

The epigraph for "Cracked" is from "Winter" from QUICK by Anne Simpson, Copyright ©2007 Anne Simpson. Reprinted by permission of McClelland and Stewart, a division of Penguin Random House Canada Limited. All rights reserved. Any third party use of this material, outside of this publication, is prohibited. Interested parties must apply directly to Penguin Random House Canada Limited for permission. Thank you to McClelland & Stewart for permission to use these lines.

"B-Flat Minor" was written in response to a comment by Paolo Pietropaolo. In *The Signature Series*, he calls B-flat minor "a Don Draper kind of man."

"Haunted" was inspired by a line overhead at a Dionne Brand reading—an Edmonton poet said to a friend, "After all the time I gave, she ghosted me"—and by Theodore Roethke's "The Waking" from *Collected Poems of Theodore Roethke*, Doubleday, 1961.

The epigraph for "For Gerda, on the threshold" is from "Beethoven: Op. 95" from *Songs for Relinquishing the Earth*, Brick Books, 2013. Thank you to Brick Books for permission to use these lines.

Details about Richard III's discovery are from "Richard III Dig: DNA Confirms Bones are King's." BBC News. *BBC News*. Feb. 4, 2013. In the battle of Bosworth Field, the Earl of Northumberland, Richard's supposed ally, kept his troops off the field. The epigraphs are from Shakespeare's "The Tragedy of Richard the Third," *The Complete Works*, General Editor Alfred Harbage, The Viking Press, 1977; and Jeanette Winterson's *The Passion*, Grove Press, 1987.

Details about Samuel Pepys are from Claire Tomalin's *Samuel Pepys: The Unequalled Self*, Vintage, 2002. The quotations from "A Diary" are taken from Samuel Pepys. *The Diary of Samuel Pepys*, Vol. 11, edited by John Warrington, Everyman's Library, 1967.

ALBERTA ADVANTAGE

"Athabasca Glacier 1924" is a response to an exhibit of Lawren Harris's and A.Y. Jackson's paintings and Byron Harmon's photographs put on by the Art Gallery of Alberta in 2014.

The italicized lines in "Big Burn" are from Samuel Pepys. *The Diary of Samuel Pepys*, Vol. 11, edited by John Warrington, Everyman's Library, 1967.

"Flood Erasures 2013" was written for *Geist*'s Erasures contest. The source text for the poem is from Rachel Lebowitz's *Cottonopolis*, Pedlar Press, 2013.

The epigraph for "Garden" is from Voltaire's *Candide*, edited by Stanley Appelbaum, Dover Publications, 1991.

Information about Kananaskis is from Ben Gadd's *Handbook of the Canadian Rockies*, Corax Press, 1995.

The epigraph for this section is from e.e. cummings' *Tulips and Chimneys*, W.W. Norton, 1923.

The information on Louisa Cody, Arta Cody, Irma Cody, Buffalo Bill Cody, and Annie Oakley is taken from the following sources:

- Buffalo Bill Historical Centre.
- Louis S. Warren. *Buffalo Bill's America: William Cody and the Wild West Show*, Vintage, 2006.
- William F. Cody and Frank Christianson. *The Life of Hon. William F. Cody, Known as Buffalo Bill*, U of Nebraska P, 2011.
- Glenda Riley. "Annie Oakley: Creating the Cowgirl." *Montana: The Magazine of Western History*, vol. 45, no. 3, 1995, 32–47.

The italicized lines in "Testimony" are from Louis S. Warren, *Buffalo Bill's America: William Cody and the Wild West Show*, Vintage, 2006.

Louisa's locket, Arta's shoes, Annie's hat and gun, and Buffalo Bill's artifacts are in the Cody Museum in Cody, Wyoming.

"Soiled Doves" was inspired by a tin token bought in a former brothel, now a store, in Jerome, Arizona. The information on the Prescott brothel is taken from an article by Michael S. Foster, John M. Lindly and Ronald F. Ryden. "The Soiled Doves of South Granite Street: The History and Archaeology of a Prescott, Arizona Brothel." *Kiva,* vol. 70, no. 4, 2005, 349–374.

The epigraph for "Lightning over Wyoming" is from Tennessee Williams' *The Glass Menagerie*, New Directions, 1999. "Lightning over

Wyoming" was written about Devils Tower National Monument, Wyoming, USA. The Lakota, Dakota and Nakota people consider the tower a sacred site. Devils Tower is also a stop on the Sturgis Bike Rally, which attracts over 500,000 bikers every August.

Acknowledgements

I would like to thank the editors who published earlier versions of some poems in the following journals.

- Edmonton Poetry Festival's website: "Elms"
- *Forage*: "Man of the West" and "Annie's Gun"
- *FreeFall*: "B-Flat Minor"
- *Grain*: "Blue Scarf" and "Lightning over Wyoming"
- *Heavy Feather Review*: "VW Ramblings"
- *Stroll of Poets Anthology 2018*: "Lament"
- *The Dalhousie Review*: "The King in the Car Park"
- *The Nashwaak Review*: "Cracked" and "A Diary"
- *The Prairie Journal*: "Soiled Doves"
- *The Windsor Review*: "Drought" and "Hinton 2013"

I am grateful to the Alberta Foundation for the Arts for its support. The grant provided by the foundation allowed me the time to write an earlier version of this manuscript.

I would like to offer my immense gratitude to Jenna Butler for her brilliant editorial suggestions. Thanks also to Douglas Hildebrand, Mat Buntin, Peter Midgley, Mary Lou Roy, Cathie Crooks, Duncan Turner, Monika Igali, and Alan Brownoff at the University of Alberta Press. I'm delighted that *Ghosts Still Linger* is part of the Robert Kroetsch Poetry Series.

"Little Sure Shot" and "Glass Targets in a Museum" were edited by Joan Crate, who made it clear what the reader needed to know. "Moose Photobomb," and "Saturday Night Prowl" were written at Sage Hill's Poetry Colloquium, 2017—thank you to Steven Heighton for his mentorship at this fantastic workshop.

"Haunted" and "For Gerda, on the Threshold" were workshopped at the Banff Writing Studio, 2019—thank you to Karen Solie, Eduardo C. Corral, and Aisha Sasha John for their insightful suggestions and encouragement.

Special thanks to my parents, my siblings—Kristy, Stuart, and Jon—and my extended family. This book is for Derrick: for his hugs, his humour, and his honesty.

Other Titles from University of Alberta Press

Fields of Light and Stone
ANGELINE SCHELLENBERG

Memory and reality, homeland and settlement, life and death—uncovering sacrifices, secrets, and forgiveness.

Robert Kroetsch Series

Memory's Daughter
ALICE MAJOR

Listen to the voices of the muses in a Scottish-Canadian daughter's homage to her parents.

A volume in cuRRents, a Canadian literature series

Little Wildheart
MICHELINE MAYLOR

Quirky, startling, earthy poems reflect the moods of existence.

Robert Kroetsch Series

More information at uap.ualberta.ca